DUDLEY PUBLIC LIBRARIES

The loan of this book may be renewed if not required by other readers, by contacting the library from which it was borrowed.

1 0 SEP 2022

1/4

OUR PLANET
OUR FUTURE

SAVING THE SEAS

Written by
Azra Limbada

BookLife
PUBLISHING

©2020
BookLife Publishing Ltd.
King's Lynn
Norfolk PE30 4LS

All rights reserved.
Printed in Malaysia.

A catalogue record for this
book is available from the
British Library.

ISBN: 978-1-83927-253-0

Written by:
Azra Limbada

Edited by:
John Wood

Designed by:
Drue Rintoul

PHOTO CREDITS

Images are courtesy of Shutterstock.com. With thanks to Getty Images, Thinkstock Photo and iStockphoto. Cover - Mr.anaked, Davdeka. 4&5 - Vadim Sadovski, Zbynek Jirousek. 6&7 - MarcelClemens, RLS Photo, Dmitry Polonskiy, Jaros, Alberto Loyo. 8&9 - Timothy Baxter, arka38, GOLFX. 10&11 - Rich Carey, Photography by Adri. 12&13 - Rich Carey, Ermolaev Alexander. 14&15 - Navapan Assavasuntakul, Alisa24. 16&17 - Rich Carey, Littlekidmoment. 18&19 - Kev Gregory, Daisy Daisy. 20&21 - Ministerie van Buitenlandse Zaken [CC BY-SA (https://creativecommons.org/licenses/by-sa/2.0)], rainyrf. 22&23 - Andrii Zastrozhnov, daizuoxin, INSAGO, umarazak.

CONTENTS

Words that look like this can be found in the glossary on page 24.

EARTH

Our planet is called Earth. Earth is about 4.5 billion years old, which is very old! Earth is home to lots of plants and animals.

EARTH

WHAT CAN YOU SEE?

Can you see the green trees and the Sun in the sky?
Can you see the starry sky and the blue seas?

BLUE WHALE

OUR WORLD IS FILLED WITH LIFE, FROM TINY FLOWERS TO THE GIANT BLUE WHALE.

WATER, WATER, EVERYWHERE!

Earth is covered in water. Water can be found in rivers and lakes, but most of Earth's water is found in oceans.

OCEAN

RIVER

LAKE

There are lots of different types of sea animals, plants and other <u>organisms</u> that live in the oceans. All of these things living in the oceans are called <u>marine</u> life!

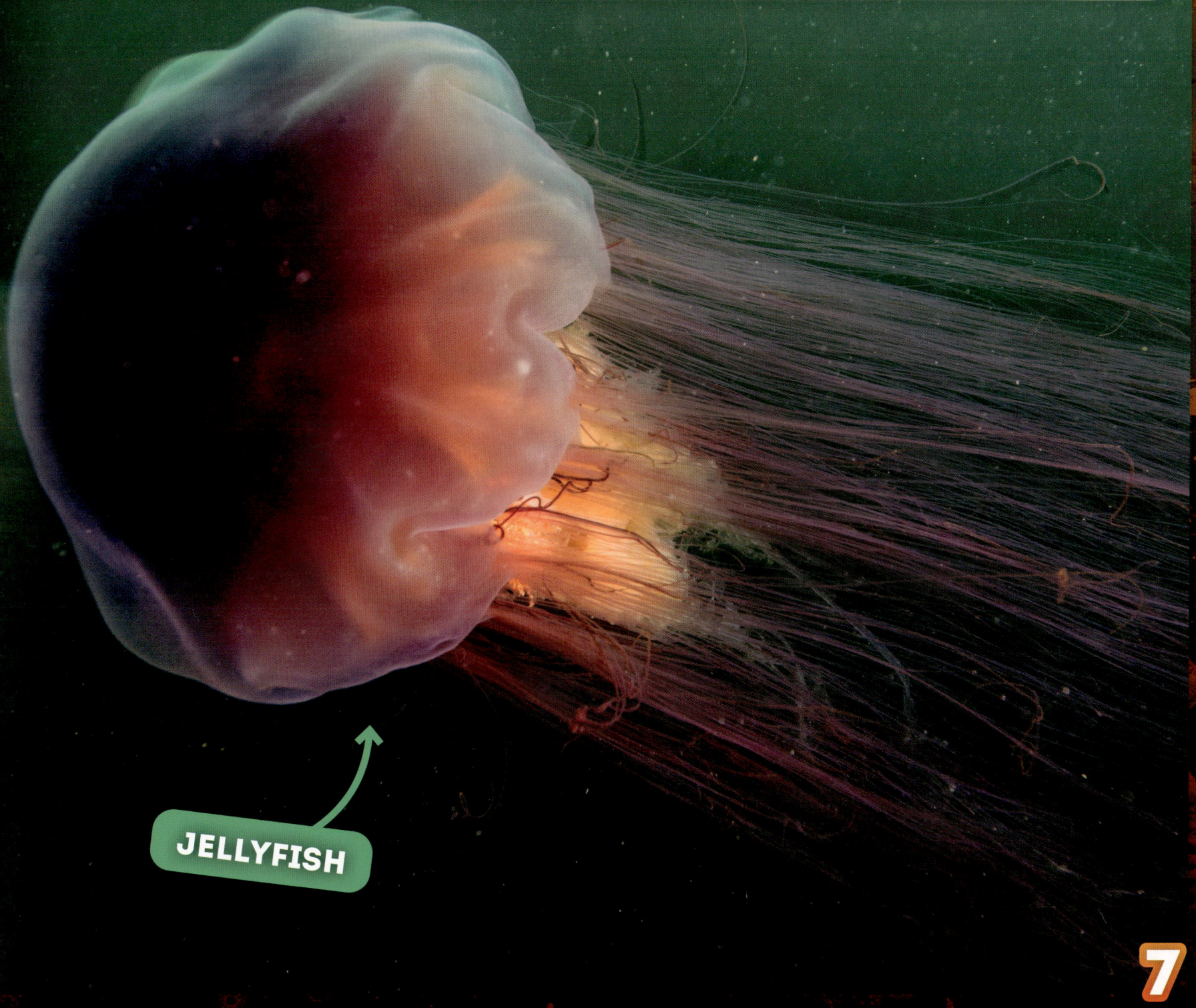

JELLYFISH

WHAT LIVES IN THE OCEAN?

Earth's oceans are filled with coral reefs. A coral reef is made up of hundreds or thousands of tiny corals. The corals stick together in different shapes and sizes.

CORAL REEF

CORAL

A coral reef makes a good home for lots of sea creatures. Fish, lobsters and seahorses all live in coral reefs!

LOOK AT THIS TINY SEAHORSE SWIMMING!

PLASTIC POLLUTION

We use plastic every day. But what happens to plastic when we have finished with it? Sadly, lots of it gets thrown into the sea.

THROWING PLASTIC IN THE SEA IS CALLED PLASTIC POLLUTION.

Lots of plastic in the ocean is harmful to sea animals. Sometimes <u>seabirds</u> get tangled up in pieces of plastic and this can hurt them.

THIS POOR GULL HAS A PLASTIC BAG STUCK AROUND ITS NECK!

SAVING THE SEA TURTLES!

One of the sea turtle's favourite foods is jellyfish. Sea turtles often think that plastic bags in the ocean are jellyfish. When they try to eat them, they can choke and die.

SEA TURTLES ARE AN ENDANGERED SPECIES. THAT MEANS THAT THEY MIGHT GO EXTINCT!

To help the sea turtles, we must stop using disposable plastic bags. Always use a reusable bag when shopping. You can also pick up plastic bags that have been thrown on the floor.

YOU CAN USUALLY RECYCLE PLASTIC BAGS AT A SUPERMARKET.

MARINE WILDLIFE

Plastic can break into very small pieces. Sometimes fish will mistake bits of plastic for food and get sick from eating it.

THESE SMALL BITS OF PLASTIC ARE CALLED MICROPLASTIC.

One way you can help is by recycling all your plastic. Lots of things around the house are made of plastic, such as yoghurt pots and drinks bottles.

IF YOU HAVE A PLASTIC TOY THAT BREAKS, SEE IF YOUR RECYCLING CENTRE CAN TAKE IT.

WHALE SHARKS

Whale sharks are endangered animals. They need our help to protect them from plastic pollution. Whale sharks might be swallowing hundreds of pieces of plastic an hour.

WHALE SHARKS ARE THE LARGEST SHARKS.

HOW CAN YOU HELP?

You can help by trying to make our planet healthy and happy. Always put rubbish properly in the bin and never throw it on the ground.

LET'S TRY TO KEEP OUR PLANET HEALTHY TOGETHER!

SAVE THE SEALS!

Sometimes young seals might see floating bits of plastic and play with it. This plastic can get wrapped around their bodies and hurt them.

THIS POOR SEAL IS TANGLED UP IN A FISHING NET.

Did you know that straws also end up in the oceans? The next time you want a drink, try having it without a straw!

MAKING THESE CHANGES WILL HELP SAVE ANIMALS IN THE SEA.

BOYAN SLAT

This is Boyan Slat. He is an inventor and wants to help keep our oceans clean. Boyan thinks of clever ways to clean the oceans. One of his ideas is a giant floating trap that catches plastic.

You can also help to clean up plastic in your area. If you live near a beach, ask your family and friends to join you on a beach clean.

WE CAN ALL WORK TOGETHER TO KEEP OUR PLANET CLEAN!

MAKE YOUR OWN RECYCLED JELLYFISH

Here's everything you need to make your own recycled jellyfish.

SCISSORS

STRING

PLASTIC BAG

BLUE FOOD COLOURING

PLASTIC BOTTLE FULL OF WATER

STEP 1: Cut the plastic bag into two sheets.

STEP 2: Gather the centre of one sheet into a small balloon to make the head. Tie it loosely with string.

STEP 3: Cut lines into the plastic below the head to make tentacles. Fill the head with a little water.

STEP 4: Put the jellyfish inside the bottle of water and add blue food colouring. Screw the lid on and shake it. Your jellyfish is ready!

GLOSSARY

disposable   something you can throw away

endangered   when a species of animal is in danger of going extinct

extinct   when a species of animal no longer exists

marine   something related to the sea

organisms   living things

pollution   when something is added to our environment that is harmful to living things

recycle   use again to make something else

seabirds   birds that visit the sea or coast often

species   a group of very similar animals or plants that can create young together

INDEX